NURSERY RHYMES

Illustrated by David Crossley

Brown Watson
ENGLAND

LITTLE BOY BLUE

Little Boy Blue,
Come blow your horn,
The sheep's in the meadow,
The cow's in the corn.

Where is the boy
Who looks after the sheep?
He's under the haystack,
Fast asleep!

SEE-SAW MARGERY DAW

See-saw Margery Daw,
Johnny shall have a new master;
He shall have but a penny a day,
Because he can't work any faster.

DOCTOR FOSTER

Doctor Foster went to Gloucester
In a shower of rain;
He stepped in a puddle,
Right up to his middle,
And never went there again.

THERE WAS AN OLD WOMAN

There was an old woman,
Who lived in a shoe,
She had so many children
She didn't know what to do;

She gave them some broth,
Without any bread,
She whipped them all soundly,
And sent them to bed.

TO MARKET, TO MARKET

To market, to market,
To buy a fat pig,
Home again, home again,
Jiggety jig.

To market, to market,
To buy a fat hog,
Home again, home again,
Jiggety jog.

BYE, BABY BUNTING

Bye, Baby Bunting,
Daddy's gone a-hunting,
Gone to get a rabbit skin
To wrap the Baby Bunting in.

HERE WE GO ROUND
THE MULBERRY BUSH

Here we go round the mulberry bush,
The mulberry bush, the mulberry bush,
Here we go round the mulberry bush,
On a cold and frosty morning.

LITTLE POLLY FLINDERS

Little Polly Flinders
Sat among the cinders,
Warming her pretty little toes;

Her mother came and caught her,
And whipped her little daughter
For spoiling her nice new clothes.

PAT-A-CAKE

Pat-a-cake, pat-a-cake, baker's man,
Bake me a cake as fast as you can;
Pat it and prick it and mark it with B,
And put it in the oven for baby and me.

HOW MANY MILES?

How many miles to Babylon?
Three score miles and ten.
Can I get there by candlelight?
Yes, and back again.
If your heels are nimble and light,
You may get there by candlelight.

MONDAY'S CHILD

Monday's child is fair of face,
Tuesday's child is full of grace,
Wednesday's child is full of woe,
Thursday's child has far to go,

Friday's child is loving and giving,
Saturday's child works hard for a living,
But the child that is born
On the Sabbath day
Is bonny and blithe, and good, and gay.

PETER, PETER

Peter, Peter, pumpkin-eater,
Had a wife and couldn't keep her;
He put her in a pumpkin shell,
And there he kept her very well.

Peter, Peter, pumpkin-eater,
Had another and didn't love her;
Peter learned to read and spell,
And then he loved her very well.

THIS LITTLE COW EATS GRASS

This little cow eats grass,
This little cow eats hay.
This little cow drinks water,
This little cow runs away.

This little cow does nothing,
Except lie down all day.
We'll chase her,
We'll chase her,
We'll chase her away!

ONE, TWO, THREE, FOUR, FIVE

One, two, three, four, five,
Once I caught a fish alive,
Six, seven, eight, nine, ten,
Then I let him go again.

Why did you let him go?
Because he bit my finger so.
Which finger did he bite?
This little finger on my right.

TINKER, TAILOR

Tinker, tailor,
Soldier, sailor,
Rich man, poor man,
Beggar man, thief.

OLD WOMAN

There was an old woman
Lived under a hill,
And if she's not gone
She lives there still.

DAYS IN THE MONTHS

Thirty days hath September,
April, June, and November;
All the rest have thirty-one.

Excepting February alone,
And that has twenty-eight days clear
And twenty-nine each leap year.

THE CUCKOO

Cuckoo, cuckoo, what do you do?
In April I open my mail;
In May I sing all day;